The Rebellion of a Rogue-Raged Economist

THE REBELLION OF A ROGUE-RAGED ECONOMIST

SANFORD KAHN

THE REBELLION OF A ROGUE-RAGED ECONOMIST

iUniverse books may be ordered through booksellers or by contacting:

iUniverse
1663 Liberty Drive
Bloomington, IN 47403
www.iuniverse.com
1-800-Authors (1-800-288-4677)

ISBN: 978-1-5320-1253-2 (sc)
ISBN: 978-1-5320-1254-9 (e)

Print information available on the last page.

iUniverse rev. date: 12/22/2016

DEDICATION

This book is dedicated to free and independent thinkers everywhere. Separate yourself from the crowd.

Sail on brothers and sisters.

Sanford Kahn, Business Author/Speaker

Long Beach, California

Sanford16@yahoo.com

PREFACE

Do you desire an economic/business book that is easy-to-read and gives a different and unique viewpoint—not the same old, same-old? Then, this is the book for you. The book is designed to challenge your mindset when it comes to the economy, business, religion and life in general.

I use a very expansive and the classical definition of economics to develop each of my concise postings. The first two postings form the basis of the book. The one on entropy is critical. No system or person can escape the Law of Entropy.

WARNING:: If you suffer from high blood pressure, you may wish to keep your medicine nearby as you read these postings. Some of these postings may aggravate an existing high blood pressure problem. Like the title says, I am a rogue economist and these posting are meant to give you a different viewpoint. It is not important to agree with these postings (that will not be a problem), but it is important to discover a different train of thought. ***Beware of what you read and hear in the popular media.***

TABLE OF CONTENTS

It goes without saying that this book has valuable content----or else I wouldn't have written it.

But, the beauty of the book is that there are no chapters that have to be read in any logical order. The book consists of a series of "economic" postings that can be read in any order. Feel free to start at the beginning, the middle or even the last posting. You might notice that some postings have been repeated in different words. I did this to drive home the importance of that particular idea.

May I suggest that you begin by reading the first two postings. They are important to understanding the nature of the book.

Now, read on!

POSTINGS

#1: KING ENTROPY RULES THE ECONOMY

What is entropy and why is it important to individuals both personally and professionally? Entropy is a measure of the disorder of a system and increases throughout the universe. All entities (this includes business, economic, government and even personal) go from a state of order to a state of disorder. This movement from order to disorder is characterized by turbulence and chaos. What this means in your personal life is that it is not a question if something will go wrong with your plans---but when. How to prepare for it? **Be as much out of debt as possible and have liquid assets.**

Notes:

#2: What is the True Definition of Economics

The modern definition of economics is the science that deals with the production, distribution, and consumption of goods and services. The modern definition transforms economics into a science--- which it isn't. The true definition of economics is the classical definition. This is that **economics is the study of human behavior in its historical setting.** In other words, economics is psychology. It can't be programmed with equations to predict human behavior. Since human behavior infuses all areas of our endeavors, economics is the closest thing to being all encompassing.

Notes:

#3: WHO OWNS THE FUTURE

The future belongs to those individuals who can quickly discern, adapt to, and exploit the unpredictable movements in the turbulent flow of life. The future doesn't belong to the Big or the Small---but to the Swift.

Notes:

#4: Is the Future Knowable?

If you understand the concept of entropy, then you must understand that the future is unknowable. The best one can do is to estimate probabilities of what might happen based on experience or history.

Notes:

#5: What is a Black Swan Event

A black swan event is one that no one expected or saw in coming. The economic ones have a large and lasting impact on the economy and the financial markets. In order to qualify for a financial black swain event three conditions are required. First, the event must be a surprised to the great majority of people. Second, it must have an acute and long lasting impact on the financial markets. Lastly, in hindsight it must appear that it was completely unpredictable. People hate to admit they were mistaken.

Notes:

#6: What is the Objective of Political Policy

The **objective** of political policy is to give individuals the incentives and opportunities to grow and prosper within the Rule of Law. This is accomplished by giving them the tax incentives to work and invest for their futures. Without new investment an economy stagnates and declines. The result will be class warfare and envy. There will be no winners and this will slowly eat away at the fabric of freedom and opportunity in American society.

Notes:

#7: WHAT IS THE KONDRATIEV WAVE?

The Kondratiev wave (K wave) is a 60 plus year cycle of economic boom and then bust. The most destructive part of the K wave occurs in the so called Winter season. In this season excess capacity is worked-off by massive debt repudiation. Commodity deflation and economic depression are the results. Politicians of any party can delay the inevitable, but can't stop it. The K wave is necessary to lay the strong foundation for vibrant economic growth that follows the Winter season. This is the Spring season in which new businesses flourish amid good economic times and rising inflation.

Notes:

#8: THE MARKETS ARE THE MASTERS

You see it really doesn't matter what I or you think. The markets are the masters. We are in a massive debt bubble that has gone well beyond the heights of 2007 and will eventually pop. The result will be a deflationary collapse that will force government to downsize for one simple reason. The revenues will not be there. The Kondratieff wave has been delayed by the central bankers, but not abolished. In the end, we will abolish our fiat currency and have one back by gold or some other commodity.

Notes:

#9: Who Are the Economic Jocks in Any Society?

The true economic jocks in any society are the entrepreneurs---the innovators. Without these creative individuals unleashing new products and services, not only American society but also all advanced societies would still be struggling back in the 1800's. They are the ones who are truly responsible for helping people improve their lives. Any society that does not reward entrepreneurship is on the path to economic suicide.

Notes:

#10: The Simple & Concise Explanation of Human Behavior

People act and do what they perceive to be in their best interest. The key word is "perception". It doesn't mean that what people do and say will always be in their best interest, but they perceive that it is. Their perception is their reality. For example, people do unselfish acts because it makes them feel good about themselves while helping others. Not a bad reason to do it.

Notes:

#11: HOW TO DESTROY OUR FUTURE

There is a saying in the Book of Proverbs that states--- **where there is no vision the people perish.** How can one have a "vision of the future" when we have a tax code that discourages work and investment? How can we have a "vision of the future" when we have no idea of what the dollar will be worth a year, five years or even longer from now. If is very difficult to make long-term financial plans when your currency bounces up and down like a yo-yo. When people lose their sense of the future, they tend to follow politicians who espouse class envy and warfare.

Notes:

#12: Business Blunder #1

Straying From Your Core Business--Don't go into a business that you know nothing about. It's foolish to branch out if your second business doesn't increase your sales significantly and adds to your Free Cash Flow. There is a wise investment saying that says "Never play another man's game". Stick with your game and play it well.

Notes:

#13: BUSINESS BLUNDER #2

Neglecting the Top Line (Sales)--Unless your sales and revenue are growing, your bottom line will eventually shrink. Think of the top line as the potential energy of the firm. The greater the potential energy of the firm the more leverage and opportunities you have to expand your market share.

Notes:

#14: Business Blunder #3

The False God of Worshipping High Profit Margins---
Many businesses, large and small, focus their attention
on the quarterly bottom line and maximizing their profit
margins. When you try to maximize your profit margins,
you will also maximize your competition. Instead of
focusing on profit margins, focus instead of increasing
your **Free Cash Flow** (FCF). This is defined as income
from operations minus capital expenditures. Use your
Free Cash Flow to innovate new products and services
to obtain additional market share.

Notes:

#15: Business Blunder #4

Financially Starving the Opportunities & Feeding the Problems—we are all victims of inertia. Old problems keep you stagnant whereas new opportunities are potentials for growth and can bring in much needed revenue and new customers.

Notes:

#16: Business Blunder #5

Planning Your Business in an Economic Vacuum –You do not live and work in an economic vacuum. You can develop the best business strategy that time and money can buy, BUT if it is not in harmony with macro economic trends, you can stumble badly.

Notes:

#17: THE FOUR POINTERS TO INCREASE YOUR HAPPINESS

1. Try to keep your commute short. For those who have experience it, driving in traffic is not only stressful but it is a different kind of hell every day.
2. You might be happier choosing more time with your family and yourself over more money. If your taxes go up and your marginal tax rate starts to approach 50%, why work for government. Take more leisure over more money. To hell with big government!
3. Watch how you spend your money. There is an abundance of data that support experiences are more rewarding than more material goods. How many toys do you need? Go to Hawaii and enjoy the beach and body surfing in warm water.
4. Be wise in using your leisure time. For example, having dinner at a nice restaurant with good friends is rewarding both socially and mentally. I personally find visiting the Polo Lounge at the Beverly Hills Hotel very rewarding and uplifting for me. It is a real show with some of the characters who walk in.

Notes:

#18: WHAT IS LIFE?

Life is simply a continuing struggle to keep money coming in and teeth and hair from falling out.

Notes:

#19: WHERE GOES THE ECONOMY

In a nutshell this is the problem. In the past 25 years total debt in the U.S. grew more than 2.5 times the economic growth of the country. This is a debt bubble—and debt bubbles always burst and they are followed by periods of austerity and deflation. The U.S. Fed can delay the process but can't stop it. In the end the markets rule.

Notes:

#20: DEBT, CONSTIPATION AND VIBRANT ECONOMIC GROWTH

Have you ever been constipated? You feel sluggish with no pep and vitality. When you finally clear-out the blockage, you feel like a new person with pep and vigor. And, so it is with the economy. The U.S. economy is constipated with too much total debt. It is putting a damper on economic growth. You can't spur economic growth by adding more debt to an already over indebted economy. The economy then gets more debt constipated. There has to be a reset and a debt catharsis to flush out the excess debt. Without this debt catharsis the economy muddles along with diminishing employment opportunities and income growth. Please realize that when (not if) this debt catharsis occurs, it will be painful process but necessary to set the stage for sustained vibrant economic recovery.

Notes:

#21: WHAT IS HISTORY'S BIGGEST LESSON?

Going back to the beginning of recorded history, the biggest lesson from history is that people don't learn from history. They make the same mistakes over and over. What is really sad is that history shows us that even the experts that know history well, don't learn from history. Witness the financial experts at the U.S. Federal Reserve who said in early 2008 that we do not have a housing bubble. The lesson should be beware of the advice from experts especially Wall Street ones.

Notes:

#22: A SIMPLE AND ENTERTAINING QUIZ

Let's say you are approached by a genie on a deserted beach and this genie will grant you only one wish that must be expressed in one word that is a noun. What would your wish be? To me the correct answer is---**Prosperity**. In the world of politics this is achieved by giving individuals the tax incentives to work and invest for their future. True prosperity is not achieved by welfare spending and tax subsides.

Notes:

#23: All you need to know about Socialism

Socialism=Slavery. The state owns and controls you.

Notes:

#24: A SIMPLE PRIMER ON TAX RATES

Once you have combined Federal and State marginal income tax rates above 50%, the individual is NOT working for themselves. They are working for government. They are becoming serfs of the state. Individuals want to work and better themselves and their families not government. Smart individuals will pick more leisure time than working. Why stress yourself out for government?

Notes:

#25: THE CONSERVATION OF PERSONAL POWER

In physics, there exists a law titled the "conservation of matter". It basically states that matter can't be easily created or destroyed. However, the states of matter can be changed. For example, by applying enough heat to a solid you can transform it into a liquid, as with ice. A liquid heated to the boiling point can be changed into a gas. In all cases, they are still the original matter but in a different state.

In a similar vein, using the law of the conservation of matter, there exists in all societies a **conservation of personal power**. It states that Personal Power can neither be created nor destroyed, but it can be transferred. The more you want government to take over the responsibility for your economic well-being, the more personal power you must transfer to it. Let this continue and eventually you will be governed by a pack of wolves.

Notes:

#26: OUR BIGGEST THREAT

For those of you feeling that global warming is the biggest threat facing the U.S., please beware of this. An enemy missile (North Korea and Iran) with a hydrogen bomb warhead detonated far above the Earth's atmosphere (electromagnetic pulse) could shut down electric grids from coast to coast in North America. These circuits are completely destroyed. There is no electricity period. Our civilization can't survive in its present form without electricity. We go back to the 1800's----your car for a horse.

Notes:

#27: One Sure Sign a Recession May be Coming

When the head of the U.S. Federal Reserve, Jenet Yellen, states that a chance of a recession is minimal, start thinking the opposite is now probable. The forecasting abilities of the Federal Reserve, both under former chairman Ben Bernanke and current chairwoman Ms. Yellen, are less accurate than throwing darts at a board. Remember Chairman Bernanke saying we do not have a housing bubble in 2007. They use computers to analyze the economy. It can't work because the economy is composed of complex human interactions that make a vibrant economy grow or decline. With Ms. Yellen's recent statement that the risk of a recession is minimal, one can be right around the corner.

Notes:

#28: CHRISTOPHER COLUMBUS AND HIS SUBSIDY

Christopher Columbus was responsible for the thinking of modern government. He didn't know where he was going when he started; he didn't know where he was when he got there; and he did it all on a Government grant. Chris did well.

Notes:

#29: Our Two Political Choices

Any society in any country has only **Two** broad economic/political choices going forward. **The First** is they can institute policies that will empower the individual—Or—**The Second** is they can succumb to policies that will empower the government. The first leads to more freedom and growing opportunities for all and the second leads to a loss of freedom and the road to serfdom.

Notes:

#30: GUN CONTROL>>>IT WON'T WORK

Liberal politicians in both the states and in various municipalities are passing strict measures to restrict gun ownership and the ammo you can buy. Will this help to reduce the homicide rate? No! A case study is the city of Chicago. Chicago has very strict regulations on gun ownership…but it reigns supreme as the murder and mayhem capital of America. The murderous violence in Chicago and other large cities is driven by the breakdown of the family unit. When children do not have a male authority figure in the household, they grow up undisciplined and wild. Until you address this problem, you will be focusing on the wrong solutions.

Notes:

#31: THE CORRUPTION OF GOVERNMENT

British Lord Acton said it best---

"Power tends to corrupt, and absolute power corrupts absolutely". Big government is not your friend; it is your competitor for personal power. Government is not interested in helping people. Above all, it is interested in maintaining its power and control. Never sacrifice your liberties for some vague promises from government.

Notes:

#32: OUR MOST PRESSING SOCIAL/ECONOMIC PROBLEM

The most pressing social/economic problem facing the U.S. is the considerable and persistent out-of-wedlock birth percentages. These children are being raised without stable families and are not taught to respect authority and to expend the attitude and effort needed for success and advancement. The net result is that they join gangs looking for an authority figure.

Notes:

#33: WHAT IS THE FATAL DISEASE OF REPUBLICS?

As Wendell Phillips once wrote: **"Debt is the fatal disease of republics, the first thing and the mightiest to undermine governments and corrupt the people."** When the debt levels of government get exceptionally large (100% of GDP or larger), it starts to act like a brake on economic growth. Taxes will have to be raised to service the debt and fund the excessive spending that leads to the higher debt levels. Raising taxes puts downward pressure on economic growth and makes the debt burden that much worse. You start to go into a "**debt death spiral**".

Notes:

#34: THE LAST REFUGE OF CHEAP POLITICIANS

Class warfare and envy is the last refuge of cheap politicians who have nothing to offer. Consider this simple equation: ***Money=Opportunity***. Money doesn't guarantee success but if you have it, it certainly improves your odds. If you tax away money (opportunity) from those who have done especially well within the Rule of Law, do you also not tax away opportunity from those who wish to advance up the economic ladder? Rising taxes and regulation are a barrier for success. You can't hurt one group without hurting others. We are all connected.

Notes:

#35: AN INSIGHTFUL CRITIQUE OF AMERICA BY OUR ENEMY

While a prisoner of war in 1946, Herman Goering (leading member of the <u>Nazi</u> party and responsible for economic planning) gave an insightful critique of America and the socialist agenda. "Your America is doing many things in the economic field which we found out caused us so much trouble. You are trying to control people's wages and prices---people's work. If you do that you must control people's lives. And no country can do that part way. I tried it and failed. Nor can any country do it all the way either. I tried that to and it failed. You are no better planners than we. I should think your economists would read what happened here. Will it be as it always has been that countries will not learn from the mistakes of others and will continue to make the mistakes of others all over again and again?"

Notes:

#36: What You Need to Know About the Future

All that one can know about the future is that it will arrive when it gets here. You can't know its shape or what it will be like. But, you can at least prepare yourself to react to its opportunities and hazards. Do not be passive. Value your freedom of movement that will allow you to profit from the opportunities presented. Don't ever sign that freedom away.

Notes:

#37: THE END—CAUGHT IN A LIQUIDITY TRAP

Central banks have tried to stimulate growth by providing an abundance of cheap money and credit. This cheap credit has created bubbles in most, if not all, investment markets. Due to this lack of high-yielding investment prospects, individuals start to hoard cash. No matter how much cheap credit central bankers throw at the economy, it mostly sits idle. This is the **Liquidity Trap** and it is an early indication that central bankers have run out of tricks to stimulate the economy. The cheap credit game is over! China is now in this position.

Notes:

#38: WHAT IS THE PURPOSE OF LIFE?

The purpose of life is to grow and prosper within the Rule of Law and the Bounds of Morality. Among human beings, the notions of growing and prospering are subjective, that is, they are individually conceived. If prospering to you means sitting on a mountaintop pondering your existence, so be it. On the other hand, you may wish to grow and prosper and add to the wealth of society by opening up a legitimate business enterprise. The latter is more preferable than the former because it adds to the wealth and well being of society.

The above paragraph begins with the phrase "the purpose of life". Many individuals who ponder their existence ask the perpetual question—what is the meaning of life? This is a difficult question to answer because they are asking the wrong question. You find meaning for your life within the context of its purpose. Define that first and then a better insight into the meaning will follow.

Notes:

#39: WHAT WILL ULTIMATELY WIN---INFLATION OR DEFLATION?

Deflation will ultimately win out. Why? Because of the massive debt build-up, both in the U.S. and other developed countries, more income will be required to pay for past debt-financed consumption at the expense of less income for current consumption. In addition, all debt bubbles Burst and deflate assets bought on debt. How can you be prepared? Be solvent and liquid.

Notes:

#40: NOTHING NEW

There is nothing new under the economic/political sun. Just different actors on stage saying this time it is different. The economic problems we face today have also been faced by other societies. Whether or not we prosper depends on the choices we make. In an electric circuit electrons take the path of least resistance. Unfortunately, societies in their economic choices also take the path of least resistance. When these policies get so far out of balance, market forces will bring them back to reality with painful consequences.

Notes:

#41: ARE YOU A SLAVE?

When you are in debt you are in essence a slave. You are beholden to the lender. Having a burdensome level of debt ties you in chains. You may have to work at a job you despise and not able to pursue your dreams. The stress of paying on the debt may also impact negatively your health and your marriage. How to be free? Pay down and off your debt, avoid bad habits like drinking to excess and smoking and avoid drugs. Only then can you happily give the middle-finger salute to the Man.

Notes:

#42: THE BASIS OF SOCIETAL WEALTH AND WELLBEING

Understanding the economy should not be complicated. To expect increases in real incomes without increases in productivity is like asking for water to flow uphill. You are asking for something that has never been and never will be. You can't have increasing productivity without policies that encourage investment, especially, new investment. New investment would be new businesses and new ways of doing things. The genesis of new investment is tax policies that encourage work and investing. Tax policies and regulations that punish work and investment will only lead to stagnation and decay. Does this sound familiar?

Notes:

#43: HOW LONG CAN IT LAST?

How long can it last? You tell me! The U.S. went completely off the gold standard on August 15, 1971. Since that important date, total debt (federal, state and private debts), has been growing at a rate of 2.5 times GDP. How much longer can this continue?

No debt bubble in history has lasted this long (thank you U.S. Federal Reserve) and has been this extreme and infected most areas of our society. This debt bubble will Burst. I will let you figure out the consequences.

Notes:

#44: THE LIMITS OF TAXATION

Politicians feel if they keep raising income tax rates, especially on the wealthy, the money will keep flowing in. Not true! There is a law of diminishing returns on raising taxes. Beyond a certain income level, the more you raise income tax rates the less revenue you will get. Let's take a real example. Gordon Brown was the prime minister of the United Kingdom from 2007 to 2010. In his last year in office he substantially raised the income tax rate for those making a million pounds (about $1.5 million U.S.) or greater. What happened? In one year those reporting incomes above a million pounds dropped 60% while the revenue to the British Treasury dropped 50%. Wealthy people know how to use the tax system to reduce their tax burden. But, more important, they can chose to enjoy more leisure and less work. When you pay high marginal income tax rates, you are working for government---not yourself. Who wants to do that?

Notes:

#45: WE LIVE AND WORK IN AN ORDERED UNIVERSE

There is no order in the universe that we live and work in. All movement in our social, economic, political and personal universes is governed by turbulence and chaos. Proof>>>just pickup a newspaper. **The Law of Entropy** guarantees this is how it is and will always be. Think about it! If everything was ordered and predictable, where would be the opportunities for success and advancement? Out of turbulence springs the opportunities for success. Also, out of turbulence come the opportunities for failure. There are no guarantees.

Notes:

#46: WHY CENTRAL PLANNING WILL ALWAYS FAIL

Modern economies are highly complex organisms. They are composed of millions of people making sundry decisions many times a day. Given this state-of-complexity, central planning implodes because no mortal can predict the future. Planners (especially government planners) always assume that past patterns always repeat themselves. They don't mainly because the economic/political universe we live and work in is governed by turbulence and chaos. The future isn't knowable to the degree central planners would like. Failure is their fate.

Notes:

#47: What is Debt?

Reduced to its basic definition, debt is borrowing. When government borrows, they are borrowing prosperity from the future to finance "free" government programs to be enjoyed now. All debt eventually has to be repaid. They can delay payment, but then the price will be larger. Unless the economy is growing faster than the rate of debt accumulation, standards of living will decline for the population. How to achieve vibrant economic growth? Through tax policies that will give individuals the strong incentives to work and invest for their futures. Add to this a strong and stable dollar.

Notes:

#48: THE IMMORALITY OF POLITICAL POLICY

When is political policy immoral? It is immoral when it purposely takes away economic opportunities and avenues for advancement for those at the lower rungs of the economic ladder. It is very unfortunate that many minority leaders (secular & religious) do not denounce government attempts to substantially increase the minimum wage. You have 30% to 40% minority youth unemployment in the bigger cities in the U.S. By substantially increasing the minimum wage, you will be locking these individuals out of entry- level jobs for unskilled labor. They will become disconnected from society. When Individuals are locked-out from legitimate employment, they will eventually take their frustrations out on society. Some may reason they have nothing to lose by not being peaceful.

Notes:

#49: The end of a game

The economic calamity in the early 1930's ushered-in the liberal social welfare state under FDR. Can it be that the next economic calamity (the bursting of the debt bubble) will usher it out? Why? The liberal social welfare entitlement state has run its course and can no longer be afforded. The U.S. national debt is starting to accelerate at a geometric rate. This is not sustainable. All games come to an end---nothing goes on forever.

Notes:

#50: Finite vs. Infinite

The actual physical resources to satisfy our almost infinite desires at any particular time are finite in nature. But, mans' imagination is infinite. You can't run out of resources that support our standard of living because of substitution and invention. For example, most people think our supply of oil in the ground is finite and will eventually run out. (I could argue differently; but that is not important). Did you ever hear of hydrogen? The fuel-celled car has already been developed by both Toyota and Hyundai. The only emissions are heat and water vapor. One other thing, hydrogen is the most abundant element in the universe. You can never run out of it.

Notes:

#51: The One Important Stock

Is it possible there can be one stock that can give you an idea of the direction of the economy? Our market economy depends on the expansion of credit for continuing growth. Synchrony Financial (symbol SYF) is a consumer financial services company. It is one of the largest issuers of credit cards, commercial credit products and consumer installment loans. If its stock is in a down trend, this would be a good indication that the economy might be stalling-out in the near future. At this moment, its stock is below its 50, 100 and 200 day moving averages. This is not a good sign. If you are in the stock market, it can't hurt to keep tract of it.

Notes:

#52: HOW TO MAKE GOD LAUGH

Tell him your plans. It not a question if something will go wrong----but when (entropy again).

Notes:

#53: How Much of What Will Make You Happy?

According to tons of basic research on the subject of happiness, getting more and more of the crap advertised on TV and the internet doesn't make you any happier or more fulfilled as a person. Once you have met your basic needs, getting more and more superfluous stuff doesn't increase your happiness. The late philosopher of the common man, Eric Hoffer said it best. He stated **it** very concisely, ***"You can never get enough of what you don't really need to make you happy."***

Notes:

#54: THE MARKETS ARE THE MASTERS>>END GAME

The financial markets have gone to extremes and we are living in a bubble economy induced by central bankers. This has resulted in extreme wealth inequality and also extreme divide politically. The last time this happened was 1929. The markets are the masters, not politicians. This will be corrected and the correction will be painful. There is nothing new in economic history.

All games come to an end including this one. The economic pendulum swings in both directions and it will correct the excess induced by both political parties. Be liquid and solvent.

Notes:

#55: SOCIALISM=THE NEW SLAVERY

What is the true and correct definition of Socialism? *Socialism is a form of government where the government controls completely or in large measure the Three Factors of Production---Land, Labor and Capital.* At best, you are a serf---at worse you are a slave. In either case, you are entangled under the yoke of government bondage. They own you and you are not free. This is not the path for our future.

Notes:

#56: WHAT IS THE TRUE DEFINITION OF RELIGION

Religion in its pure form is a spiritual relationship between the individual and the Creator. Now, go back and read this definition again. Where in this definition is there any mention of the word "institution"? There isn't any. True religion is individually based not institutionally based. When you institutionally organize a religion, it slowly devolves into power and control. It tends to become corrupt. True religion is about a spiritual connection and man-made institutional religion is about power and control. They are opposite of each other.

Notes:

#57: The Art of Defining Your Beliefs

There is One thing you must never do when defining your beliefs and what is important to you. You must Never, Never let any institutional religion tell you what to **Do, Say and Think**. You are the pilot of your own ship; you set the course. They should have no control over you. Once you set the course, you then have to take the responsibility for your actions.

Notes:

#58: KNOW THE DISASTER FORMULA

What is the disaster formula? Remember this formula: ***Debt + Deflation=Disaster***. When both individuals and societies pile debt onto more debt in the midst of deflationary forces, the result will be debt liquidation and a rise in bankruptcies. The economy then goes into a deflationary death spiral until the total debt is brought back into normal and sustainable ranges. This is what the Federal Reserve in the U.S. and other central bankers are trying to avoid. In the end, they will lose. Why? Because the massive amount of unsustainable debt creates its own deflationary force. There are NO free lunches!

Notes:

#59: How Bubbles End

Bubbles burst when sellers ask for an inflated price for their asset and buyers refused to make a bid. The financial "house of cards" that was built on ever rising prices then collapses. What goes up rapidly in price then collapses rapidly in price also. There really doesn't have to be any particular reason why the bubble burst. The asset price just got so far out of line that it could not be sustained anymore. The financial pendulum swings in both directions. The further it goes to an extreme in one direction the more potential energy it has to swing to an extreme in the opposite direction. The financial pendulum never stops.

Notes:

#60: HAPPINESS: ACCEPTING RISK IN LIFE

First, it is important to realize that **all investment is speculation**. The only difference is that some people will admit it and others are delusional and think there is a difference. Let's take two examples of the bluest of the blue chip stocks. Years ago General Motors was considered a first-rate blue chip stock. Nothing could go wrong with GM. Well, you know what happened to GM's stock. The company went bankrupt and the existing shareholders were wiped out. Another example of a blue chip stock is IBM. Yet from 1970 to 1995 IBM's stock went nowhere while the market went up. There are other examples, but I think you get my point. If you wish to prosper (personally or professionally) then you have to expose yourself to risk.

Notes:

#61: WHAT SHOULD BE THE PRIMARY FOCUS OF YOUR BUSINESS

The primary focus of your business should be to increase its **Free Cash Flow**. Free cash flow is defined as income from operations minus capital expenditures. Free Cash Flow is the wherewithal, the stuff, that successful business people can use to innovate new products and services. It becomes a tool to grab market share from your competitors. With it you become adroit and swift and you can react successfully to the changing market forces.

Notes:

#62: THE NATURE OF CAPITALISM

Capitalism without liberties and the access to open markets can lead to an entrenched wealthy class and a loss of opportunities. Capitalism is fluid and dynamic whereas socialism is stagnation. What do you expect from a government controlled economy? Overtime, stagnation leads to decay, decline and corruption.

Notes:

#63: How to Measure Stock Market Risk

According to Warren Buffett, the percentage of total market capitalization as a percent of the the US GDP is "probably the best single measure of where valuations stand at any given moment." When the percent is greater than 115%, the stock market is significantly overvalued. From the opposite perspective, when the ratio is below 50% the stock market is significantly undervalued. You can find where the ratio stands on any particular trading day by going to http://www.gurufocus.com/ and click on "market".

Notes:

#64: A New Word to Describe Our Times

There is a new word you should know that describes our political times and the leadership that represents it. The word is "***kakistocracy***". The definition of kakistrcracy is government by the worst persons; a form of government in which the worst persons are in power or want to be in power. The western world is lacking leadership and vision.

Notes:

#65: How to Destroy a Society

From John Maynard Keynes—"There is no subtler, no surer means of overturning the existing basis of society than to **debauch (corrupt) the currency**." What the hell are central banks doing globally today? You do not create real economic wealth by debasing your currency. How can individuals plan for their future when they have no idea what the value of their currency will be a year, five years or even ten years from now. No wonder the middle class in shrinking.

Notes:

#66: WISHING FOR THE IMPOSSIBLE

You can't have increasing standards-of-living when productivity in the economy is negative. If you think you can, you are wishing for something that has never been and will never be. Wishing for increasing standards-of-living when productivity is negative is like wishing for water to flow up hill. As this book is being written, we have had three consecutive quarterly drops (gone negative) in productivity. Standards-of-living, including the middle class, will continue to deteriorate.

Notes:

#67: How Good of an Investment Has Residential Real Estate Been?

Well surprise! The answer is it hasn't been that good over the long-term. Financier Michael Milken did research going back to 1890 showing that the real return (after inflation) on houses was barely above zero. If you throw in the commission costs of buying and selling, that number now goes negative. For stocks it is different. They have enjoyed a real return of 6% annually over the same time period. Over the long-term, real wealth was amassed in the stock market especially with good paying dividend stocks.

Notes:

#68: Under "Rules for Radicals" by Sol Alinsky there are 8 levels of control that must be obtained before you are able to create a Socialist/ Communist State. The first is the most important.

1. Healthcare: "Control Healthcare and you control the People"
2. Poverty: Increase the Poverty level as high as possible." Poor People are easier to control and will not fight back if the government is providing everything for them to live
3. Debt: Increase the National Debt to an unsustainable level." That way you are able to increase Taxes, and this will produce more Poverty
4. Gun Control: Remove the ability to defend themselves from the Government. That way you are able to create a Police State - total local control
5. Welfare: Take control of every aspect of their lives (Food, Livestock, Housing, and Income)
6. Education: Take control of what People read & listen to; take control of what Children learn in School

7. Religion: Remove faith in God as noted in our Constitution from the Government and Schools

8. Class Warfare: Divide the People into the Wealthy against the Poor. Racially divide. This will cause more discontent and it will be easier to Tax the Wealthy with full support of the voting Poor.

Notes:

#69: WHAT IS GREED?

Greed is irrational acquisitiveness gone haywire and out-of-control. It is irrational because all sense of risk and consequences are thrown out the window. Sanity does not exist. A simple rule to remember is that if you want less, you will go home with more.

Notes:

#70: AUGUST 15, 1971—A DAY THAT WILL LIVE IN ECONOMIC INFAMY

Even I have to admit I am being somewhat dramatic in that statement. But, the date is important. If you can point to one date where our economic problems began, it would be that date. On that date, President Richard Nixon severed the last linkage the dollar had to gold. The dollar became a true fiat currency backed by the full faith and credit of U.S. politicians. Scary! Politicians could go wild on spending and balloon the national debt to pay for it without the restraint of gold being called away. Once they got the hang of it, there was no stopping them. But all games come to an end including this one. The debt bubble will eventually pop and induce a deflationary collapse. At that point, we will return to a commodity (gold for example) based currency.

Notes:

#71: How to play the Debt Game

If you are an individual or a company, may I suggest paying down a good part of your debt load. With a diminished debt load your balance sheet strengthens and you can survive the financial storms that plague all individuals and companies. It is not a question of if a financial tsunami hits but when. In addition, as you pay down your debt load, your credit score increases and it will be easier to borrow in the future at a lower rate.

Liquidity is King….. Not Elvis.

Notes:

#72: On Religion and Making Money

It is very unlikely that God's plan for the universe includes making you rich and successful. There is no evidence that this supreme being gives a hoot whether you die rich or poor. Your success depends on the actions or inactions you take. Life is risk! Good fortune favors the Bold. There is no security in playing it safe.

Notes:

#73: THE DIFFERENCE BETWEEN AND RECESSION, DEPRESSION AND A PANIC

A recession is a period in which you tighten your belt. A depression is a time in which you have no belt to tighten. And when you have no trousers to hold up, that is a panic.

Notes:

#74: What is the Greatest Destroyer of Wealth?

The greatest destroyer of Wealth & Prosperity is inept government policies that destroy the incentives to Work and Invest for one's future. You can recognize this trend by cheap politicians who want to play the class envy and warfare game. They have nothing to offer except higher taxes on the most successful and productive individuals in our society. The more you tax those who have prospered within the Rule-of-Law, the less wealth and employment opportunities will be generated. Unfortunately, the U.S. has arrived at this point.

Notes:

#75: WHAT IS THE ROADBLOCK TO REDUCING POVERTY IN THE U.S.?

The U.S. will Not make a dent in its poverty rate until it makes a substantial reduction in its illegitimacy rate. This is a moral problem that has to be solved by the leaders (both secular and spiritual) in the local communities and not by our political leaders in Washington.

Notes:

#76: Is Commercial Real Estate in a Bubble?

Is commercial real estate in a bubble? Yes, you bet it is. It is in a massive bubble. From the most recent trough in 2009, it has surged 95% in price. In the great real estate bubble of 2001-2007 it surged "only" 81%. This bubble like the last one will pop and will drag down not only commercial real estate prices but also residential property prices. Markets are linked together and do not exist in isolation.

Notes:

#77: WHY BUY THE DIVIDEND ARISTOCRATS?

First, the dividend aristocrats are 50 corporations in the S&P 500 index that have increased their dividends for at least 25 consecutive years. Since the March, 2009 bear market low, the S&P 500 index has risen 197%. The dividend aristocrats have handily beat this by rising 248% in the same time period. Nothing is cast in concrete, but this shows companies that consistently increase their dividends have a better tendency of beating the broad market. You can find a list of the dividend aristocrats at: https://investorjunkie.com/3974/dividend-aristocrats/

Notes:

#78: The rules of dating

These are the Rules of Dating<><>Rule #1: There are NO rules except what you both agree to. Rule #2: Go back and read Rule #1. Keep life simple. The more complicated you make life; the more you set yourself up for failure.

Notes:

#79: Chaos & turbulence rule

In business and in life all conditions are temporary. Nothing stays the same, nothing remains static. There is no such thing as balance in the business of life. All movement in the course of human events is governed by turbulence and chaos. There is no balance only movement seeking balance. To be in balanced is to be stagnant. **Stagnation over time produces nothing but decline and decay.**

Notes:

#80: CAN MORTALS BE PERFECT?

Mortals can't be perfect. We are not designed that way. You might say this by definition. Only God (however you define it) is perfect.

When mortals try to be perfect the result will be nothing but problems and potential disaster. Why? There is an old Greek saying that explains why the path of perfection for mortals leads to disaster. It is: for whom the Gods will destroy they first make overconfident. When individuals are overconfident they charge ahead oblivious to the dangers and crosscurrents that await. In other words, they are oblivious to the consequences (risks) of their actions. While mortals can't be perfect they can be better. As Ben Franklin noted centuries ago—best is the enemy of better.

Notes:

#81: THE REAL PROBLEM FACING OUR ECONOMIC FUTURE

From the U.S. Congressional Budget Office::"Some 85 cents of every increased dollar of spending over the next 10 years will flow to entitlements, namely health care." This leaves very little or nothing for defense (defending the country), repairing infrastructure, basic research and you fill in the rest. No matter what your political persuasion is there is no way this trend can continue. Something has to give. We can't tax ourselves out of this hole. Real budgetary reform is imperative, but unfortunately politicians will delay the inevitable until their backs are against the wall and we are facing economic calamity.

Notes:

#82: IS GOD A TYRANT?

God is no tyrant. He enforces no preordained plan for the conduct of human affairs but, instead, has bestowed upon the people the power to create a heaven or hell on Earth. Whether man thrives or perishes is dependent on the choices he makes.

This precept may be controversial and even heretical to those who believe in some divine plan for mankind. There is a divine plan but it is so simple it flies over the heads of the majority of mankind. The plan is—**there is no plan, only the one you create**. You are the helmsman of your own ship. You set the course and take the responsibility for the consequences of your actions.

Notes:

#83: WHAT IS YOUR ECONOMIC/ POLITICAL ENDOWMENT?

As an individual, you are endowed to walk and live in the light of Liberty and not be entangled under the yoke of the state. Beware of ceding too much power to the state. The state can't be trusted. Their purposes and yours are diametrically opposed. Their goal is to capture as much power and control over you as possible. Your objective is to be free and to set your own goals and priorities. Do you notice the inherent conflict-of-interest? You are the helmsman of your own ship; guide it well.

Notes:

#84: THE WEALTH OF SOCIETY & CONCEIT

The Wealth of Society can't be transferred if the transfer also destroys the incentive to produce wealth. The consequence of this action will be to make everyone poorer. In America, we believe that we are an exceptional nation—and we are. The problem, though, is that this exceptional belief leads us to the conclusion that we are impervious to the forces that made other nations fall. *We are NOT!* Sooner or later, this conceit or arrogance brings every great nation to its knees. You can't escape reality.

Notes:

#85: HOW TO SCREW MINORITIES

It is very unfortunate that many minority leaders (secular & religious) do not denounce government attempts to substantially increase the minimum wage. Increasing the minimum wage will put the least productive, lowest-skilled workers out of a job. Worse yet, it will slam the door shut for employment opportunities for these individuals. How do you reduce 30% to 40% minority youth unemployment by increasing the minimum wage? You can't!

Notes:

#86: THE THREE THINGS YOU ARE ENTITLED TO ARE.....

As an American, you are entitled to these three things: Life, Liberty and "The Pursuit of Your Happiness". Outside of this, you build and construct your own entitlements. What the government gives you, it can also take it away. Be dependent on yourself.

Notes:

#87: Sheep vs. Wolves

A nation of sheep will be governed by a pack of wolves. Guard your Liberties well. They are the bulwark that protects you from the tyrannies of the state.

Notes:

#88: HOW TO EVALUATE THE STOCK MARKET

According to stock market and investor guru, Warren Buffett, the percentage of total market cap (TMC) relative to the US GDP is "***probably the best single measure of where valuations stand at any given moment.***" Where do you find information on this leading measure of stock market evaluation? Simple! Just go to http://www.gurufocus.com/stock-market-valuations.php. The chart on the right hand side gives you a graph of this ratio going back to 1971. I would encourage you to seriously consider using this important tool.

Notes:

#89: THE MOTHER OF ALL BUBBLES

The mother of all debt bubbles is the government debt bubble. Approximately $16 trillion of government bonds worldwide now have negative yields. In 5,000 years of recorded human history this has never happened. There are no free lunches and this experiment by central bankers is producing some very negative and corrosive consequences. Very low interest rates encourage reckless governments to go on a spending spree that they can ill afford. Secondly, you are punishing thrift and killing the incentives of individuals to save for their future. This is just not wrong but borders on being immoral.

Notes:

#90: What is the ONE Condition man can't tolerate for a prolonged period of time?

Be very careful of my words. I said "tolerate". I do not mean he doesn't like it. He does like it. This one condition is "**prolong periods of prosperity**". Crazy-NO! When economic prosperity continues for a prolonged period of time, individuals will leverage (debt) it for a greater return. Eventually, the debt burden is growing faster than the incomes to support it. The debt bubble then bursts and the system implodes. A painful period of debt deleveraging and deflation then results. This will purge the system of excesses and set the stage for the next business expansion. So gives rise to the Business Cycle.

Notes:

#91: What is the cardinal rule of investing?

The cardinal rule of investing is never play another man's game. Even if this game is producing good returns but you feel it is not suitable for you, find your own game and play it well.

Notes:

#92: There is nothing new

There is nothing new under the economic/political sun. Just different actors saying this time it is different. For example, if you want a growing vibrant economy with expanding opportunities for all, then you must have tax policies that give individuals the incentives to work, save and invest for their futures. Bad economic policies, even for the best of reasons, will lead to a bad economy. There are no free lunches.

Notes:

#93: THE WAR ON PROSPERITY

The War on Prosperity! The Federal Govt. is waging war on the true engines of prosperity through high taxes and over regulation. The true engines of growth and prosperity are the entrepreneurs (small businesses). Small businesses account for two-thirds of net new employment in the U.S. and they are the future of our country. The tax code should reward success not punish it.

Notes:

#94: WHEREIN LIES A SECURE FUTURE?

Wherein lies a secure future? A secure future lies in vibrant economic growth. The genesis of vibrant economic growth are tax policies that encourage work, saving and investment, namely, entrepreneurship. Don't make life complicated---it is just that simple.

Notes:

#95: NOTHING LASTS FOREVER

The late respected economist Herbert Stein once stated that **"If something cannot go on forever, it will stop."** This applies to the financial bubbles that are being created by ultra loose monetary policies by the U.S. Federal Reserve. This game can't go on forever and it will stop. When it does the financial pendulum will swing in the opposite direction and unleash powerful deflationary forces. There are no free lunches.

Notes:

#96: THE 5 WAYS OF CREATING TRUE WEALTH

How is True Wealth created in Any society? We tend to think that because we are living in a so-called "modern times" that things are different. Not true! There are Only 5 ways to create true wealth in any society in any time period. It does not matter if the time period was two thousand years ago, today or two thousand years in the future, there will only be these five industries. These Five are: **Fishing, Mining, Agriculture, Construction and Manufacturing.** But wait! What about the service economy? Without these five there is no service economy.

The true wealth of a society comes from its ability to Produce NOT consume. Unfortunately, in the United States, the tax laws discourage production and entrepreneurship. Result=a slow growth economy.

Notes:

#97: THE POSITIVE MENTAL ATTITUDE MYTH

Both our economic and social environments are in constant motion. This motion is both turbulent and chaotic (remember entropy). If our environment is in constant turbulent motion, how could you always maintain a positive mental attitude? You simply can't. Mortals are not designed that way. Your attitude, like our environment, is always in motion. Then, if attitude is not the most important criterion of success and advancement, what is? The primary criterion that separates success from failure is action, namely positive action. Your attitude or state-of-mind can be in the gutter. <u>So what!</u> Nothing stays the same forever. Take the necessary positive actions to build value both personally and professionally. Good fortune favors the bold. **<u>Attitude follows action.</u>**

Notes:

#98: Why Plans FAIL– The Law of Failure

The law of planning states that the probability of any plan or strategy will fail is directly proportional to the square of its complexity. The old saying of **"keeping it simple"** has merit especially now in the internet age. When arguing with individuals and they say "the problem is more complex than that", it usually means it is not and they have no counter argument.

Notes:

#99: In investing never do this

Never (I repeat never) leverage an appreciating asset to buy a depreciating asset. For example, taking out a home equity loan to purchase a new car or taking an expensive vacation may sound enticing, but you are putting your asset at risk of loss if things don't work out as planned. If you go back and read the write-up on entropy, things have a habit of not working out as planned.

Notes:

#100: Approaching time=zero: The ticking debt bomb

I would like to thank Harry Dent for the following information and research. The total true debt of the United States is $130 trillion. This includes all state, Federal and private debt plus the unfunded liabilities of the Federal government. This figure now represents 707% debt to GDP ratio. For comparison purposes, at the height of World War II the ratio stood at "only" 112.7%. How much larger could the debt bubble get before it implodes?

Notes:

#101: FISCAL POLICY VS. MONETARY POLICY

The policy levers of economic growth are the function of fiscal policy, namely, policies of taxing and spending. Monetary policy, as instituted by the U.S. Federal Reserve, should only be concerned with one and only one thing. This is price stability and maintaining the value of the dollar. When you try to force economic growth by monetary policy the result is the creation of financial bubbles everywhere, especially in the bond market. This game will end badly.

Notes:

#102: DON'T BANK ON HOPE

When the ship starts to sink, don't pray. Jump! If you wait for sagging ventures to improve, you are doomed to frequent disappointment and monetary pain.

Notes:

#103: Who are the New Business Lords?

The new business lords are those individuals who can quickly discern, adapt to, and exploit the unpredictable movements in the turbulent flow of life. The new business lords will have as their goal of growing the **free cash flow** of their respective businesses.

Notes:

#104: RETURN TO GOLD?

No matter what their political persuasion, politicians will always want to spend your money through increasing taxation and more importantly through borrowing. Eventually, they run-up the debt levels of their country to unsustainable levels and the mountain of debt collapses. For 5000 years the only true restraint on the excesses of government spending is linking the currency to gold. The benefit of gold is that it ties the currency to the earth. The currency becomes grounded. In the end, we will have to return to a gold standard as the final restraint on the excesses of politicians. What this means is that the political leaders will have to prioritize their spending habits. Going further, the paramount responsibility of the U.S. Federal government is national defense and the security of the country.

Notes:

#105: RETURN TO GOLD #2

I need to explain some things about my last posting. There is No Way we can go to the gold backing of the U.S. dollar now. We are in a major financial bubble engineered by the U.S. Federal Reserve. All bubbles Burst--period. When this bubble bursts, the result will be an extreme unwinding of the debt bubble resulting in a deflationary spiral and a purge of the excesses in the economy. When it has finally run its course, only then can we return to a gold standard for the dollar. This will set the stage for the next economic upswing that will take the U.S. economy to new levels of prosperity, wealth, and innovation.

Notes:

#106: WHAT IS THE PURPOSE OF ANY INVESTMENT?

The purpose of ANY investment is to increase one's net worth. The term "net worth" applies to more than stocks, bonds, or real estate. You, your family, and your community can also be viewed as an investment.

Thinking in terms of increasing one's net worth forces individuals to expand their time horizons. What actions can I take today that will increase my net worth or value over the next 5 to 10 years? For example, why do individuals invest their time and money in going to college or trade school? Obviously, they are not making significant monies while attending school. But, they are learning a particular profession or trade (skills) that will increase their Net Worth or value in the marketplace. By so doing, individuals have the potential of increasing their incomes in the future.

Notes:

#107: WHAT IS THE ETERNAL TRUTH OF THE UNIVERSE?

The eternal truth of the universe is that all actions provoke reactions. In human terms these reactions or consequences may be positive or negative. Someone or something has to pay a price or cost. There are no free lunches.

For example, in interpersonal relationships, honest communication is both important and essential. You can control the "what and when" of your communication, but you can't control the resulting impact (positive or negative) it has on the other person. This is the cost or price of your communication.

Another example—in economics you can't simultaneously control the cost and quantity of any product or service. If you try to control the cost (price controls), the quantity (and quality) decreases. This is the result of trying to control the price of any product or service.

There are always consequences or costs to any action taken by an individual and their consequences have to be weighed against the cost of the proposed action.

Notes:

#108: Robbing Peter to pay Paul

The great Irish playwright George Bernard Shaw stated, **"A government that robs Peter to pay Paul can always depend on the support of Paul."** When working individuals pay state and Federal combined marginal income tax rates above 50%, they are not working for themselves. They are working for big government. Then the question becomes---why work. They will decide working doesn't pay and chose more leisure over working. Income tax revenues then decrease. This is the fatal flaw of democracies and the expanding entitlement state.

Notes:

#109: Definition of a Financial Salesman

How do you define a financial salesman? **A financial salesman is a used car salesman in a fancy suite.** This is especially true if they want to sell you a financial product or service where they derive a commission. Only you can answer the question is this product or service is in my best interest? You should always be distrustful of people in the financial field. They may not (and probably will not) have your best interests in mind.

Notes:

#110: WHY BE NICE?

This is a continuation of the post regarding the definition of a financial salesman. In life when you meet a stranger it is considered civil to be nice to the person. This rule does not pertain to those engaging in selling you a financial product. Being nice puts you at a disadvantage. They are after your money and Wall Street doesn't give a hoot about being nice or even honest with you. This is how you should behave towards them. **You do not have to be nice just beware of how bad you are treating them.** This will put them on the defensive and you on the offensive. You will then be in control.

Notes:

#111: WE ARE PART OF THE FINANCIAL EQUATION

Geographically the USA is touched by only the oceans and Canada and Mexico. But financially, it is touched by every country on earth. We can't retreat into fortress America.

Notes:

#112: WHY IS THERE ETERNAL CONFLICT ON A PERSONAL LEVEL?

Why is there anxiety and eternal conflict on a personal level? The human mind is an order seeking mechanism. It likes and craves order in the universe. But, there is no order in the universe (again see entropy). The world we live and work in is governed by turbulence and chaos. The result when these two different worlds collide (the mind seeking order and the real world) is anxiety, fear, depression and personal conflict. It is in this type of environment you have the best opportunities for growth and prosperity. (Please note: can you see why many individuals seek the comfort of institutional religion. It gives them a sense of order in their lives and universe. Of course, there is no order just movement governed by turbulence).

Notes:

#113: THE GATEKEEPER: THE LIGHTS OF LIBERTY AND FREEDOM

The United States is the gatekeeper of the lights of liberty and freedom. If the lights of liberty and freedom go out in the United States, they will eventually be extinguished worldwide. Beware of the enticements and promises of big and growing government. The bigger government grows the smaller your significance will be to the state. In the end, we all will be serfs of the state. There are No free lunches!

Notes:

#114: Your personal safety in the age of terrorism

The best defense against domestic terrorist attacks is armed and trained lawful citizens. The police do their best but they come after the fact. The individual is the first line of defense. Taking guns away from lawful citizens will leave us all less secure in our daily lives.

Notes:

#115: THE DESTRUCTION OF YOUR ECONOMIC SHIP

You are the pilot of your own ship. You set the course, but there are economic forces building that can wreak havoc with your plans. You have no control over these forces but you can prepare yourself from their destructive force. The forces I am talking about are the consequences from the bursting of the massive worldwide debt bubble and the resulting deflationary spiral. Your goal is to keep your economic ship afloat and sailing into the rising sun. You accomplish this by restricting your debt leverage (reducing your debt levels) and focusing on building your free cash flow in both your personal and business lives. By so doing, you will be in a better position to profit from the unfolding opportunities.

Notes:

#116: THE CONFISCATION OF WEALTH

The death tax, otherwise known as the inheritance tax, is pure and simple a confiscation of wealth. The tax is basically immoral because it taxes assets that have already been taxed at least once when they were first earned. It punishes a lifetime of investment and thrift. No sane individual will save and invest to build an estate for their children and grandchildren knowing upon death they will have to turn at least 50% over to politicians to spend. The death tax should be abolished and the monies should remain in the private economy.

Notes:

#117: WHAT IS MONEY?

Money is a store of value. It is not some commodity to be manipulated by politicians and central bankers for political purposes. How can individuals and businesses plan and invest for the future if they have no idea of what the value of money will be? A profitable investment today could be a loser in the future depending of the value of a country's currency. That is why for over 5,000 years governments have tied their currency to a commodity---usually gold. Not only does a gold backing of the currency ground the currency to the earth, but it also takes power away from central bankers and politicians. No system is perfect, but this is a vast improvement over the fiat currency we now have.

Notes:

#118: HOW TO INVEST IN THE STOCK MARKET

Please understand that investing in the stock market is risk. Stocks fall! In a bear market they can easily fall 50% or more. Your focus should be on generating current income. The stock market goes up, down or sideways, but funds paid out as a dividends represent a real return that you can actually spend. Capital gains can evaporate in a single trading day. In other words, focus your investments on companies that have been paying consistent and increasing dividends for years.

Notes:

#119: WHO RULES THE FINANCIAL MARKETS?

We like to think that Wall Street and the central bankers rule the financial markets. But, they do not! The financial markets themselves are the masters. In the end they rule and impose discipline on the excesses of the politicians and central bankers. Politicians and central bankers can delay the inevitable, but they can't stop it. The longer they delay the consequences of their excesses the more severe will be the punishment. There are no free lunches and all actions have consequences.

Notes:

#120: The worshiping of technology

When technology is placed on a pedestal and worshiped as an idol, it is no longer life-enhancing, but becomes soul-wrecking. When humans start to value things, no matter how intelligent and clever they are over other people, they are starting on the road to ruin. The survival of the human species is based on human interaction. Take that away and humans may not remain the dominate species.

Notes:

#121: THE FOLLY OF CLASS WARFARE

The resultant folly of class warfare is if you tax away money (which is opportunity) from those who have made it, do you not also tax Opportunity away from those who wish to make it? You can't hurt one without hurting the other. High taxes and over regulation is a roadblock to upward movement and prosperity.

Notes:

#122: What is the wellspring of human progress?

The wellspring of innovation and human progress comes from the genius of individuals and Not from the dictates of government elites.

Notes:

#123: WHY CENTRALLY PLANNED ECONOMIES FAIL?

Central planned economies fail for one very simple reason in that central planners can't predict the future. They make the false assumption that past trends will continue into the future. No trend last forever. Things change and sometimes abruptly.

Notes:

#124: THE MIDDLE CLASS GETS SCREWED

Any tax increase imposed on high earning taxpayers the incidence of the increase will fall on the middle class. The tax increase will lead to a loss of new investment and business creation. The result will be a loss of job creation and upward mobility. It is always the same. Class warfare and envy only shrink the economic pie. Beware of politicians who play this losing game.

Notes:

#125: WHAT IS POLITICAL HEAVEN?

Political heaven= a smaller government.

Notes:

The next two posting are especially important

#126: THE FIRST LAW OF ECONOMIC THERMODYNAMICS

The first law of thermodynamics states that energy can be changed from one form to another, but it can't be created or destroyed. In a similar vein, the **first law of economic thermodynamics** states that the amount of political power we have to shape our future is constant. We can institute policies that will make the economic pie bigger or policies that will just transfer the slices and the economic pie shrinks. There are No other choices.

Notes:

#127: The Second Law of Economic Thermodynamics

The second law of thermodynamics states that "in all energy exchanges, if no energy enters or leaves the system, the potential energy of the state will always be less than that of the initial state." Now think of our economy as a complex system or state. **The second law of economic thermodynamics** states that if we do not add energy to our economic system by giving individuals (entrepreneurs) the tax incentives to work and invest in new businesses, the potential energy (opportunities for success and advancement) will decline. The worst thing politicians can do is to raise taxes. Why---because that will rapidly suck energy out of the economic system. The result will be an economy that, at best, stagnates and, at worst, enters a precipitous decline.

Notes:

#128: The stupidity of Central Bankers

Major economies that use their central bankers to devalue their currencies to promote economic growth will only impoverish their people. It is a deadly spiral to the bottom. There will be no winners.

Notes:

#129: THE NEXT RECESSION

Every single presidential election that follows a two-termed president in the last 100 years has seen a recession in the subsequent twelve months. The greater the debt bubble in the economy the greater the downturn.

Notes:

#130: Sir Isaac Newton and Understanding Mankind

The great English physicist and mathematician, Sir Isaac Newton, understood mankind very well. He stated---**"I can calculate the motion of heavenly bodies, but not the madness of people."**

Notes:

#131: MONEY=OPPORTUNITY

Remember the above equation because it is important with regards to taxation. The more you increase taxes on those who have done well (within the Rule of Law), the more you tax away opportunity from those who wish to do well. You can't hurt one without hurting the other. To put it in another way---the more you tax away opportunity from those who have prospered, the more your tax away the opportunities from those who wish to climb the ladder of success. This is why class warfare and envy can't work in the U.S. The **GOAL** is to make the economic pie larger---not shrink it by taxing away opportunities from those who wish to better themselves.

Notes:

#132: HOW EFFECTIVE HAS BEEN SOCIAL WELFARE SPENDING?

Let's examine social welfare spending with regards to the black community. In the early 1960's before President Johnson's Great society program, 40% of blacks had their own business. Also, 87% of black families were two-parent. Let us fast forward to today. Today, less than 7% of blacks own their own business and only 25% of black families are two-parent. The social welfare system was a disaster not only on the black family structure, but also on society as a whole. **The Federal government can't erase poverty just by throwing money at it.**

Notes:

#133: HOW TO REFORM EDUCATION

You will never reform education by throwing more money at it. The more money you throw at education the less incentive the educational establishment has to reform itself. Education doesn't need more money; it needs more competition..... namely vouchers and charter schools. Parents should have the final say as to where they can send their children for the best education whether it is public, private or parochial schools.

Notes:

#134: THE POVERTY MACHINE

The careers of modern liberal progressives are absolutely dependent on keeping people in poverty. If numerous people should escape poverty, then there would be no need for more federal programs and bureaucracy to fight poverty. Think about how many careers would be threatened if poverty was eliminated.

Notes:

#135: WHAT MIDDLE CLASS?

What is the average household income if you eliminate the top 10% of households (the affluent). It is $32,352. Income wise the middle class is hurting. With high rents and high health insurance costs sucking-up income, it is no wonder the economy just limps along.

Notes:

#136: The False God of Worshipping High Profit Margins

Many businesses, large and small, focus their attention on the quarterly bottom line and maximizing their profit margins. When you try to maximize your profit margins, you will also maximize your competition. Instead of focusing on profit margins, focus instead of increasing your **Free Cash Flow** (FCF). This is defined as income from operations minus capital expenditures. Use your Free Cash Flow to innovate new products and services to obtain additional market share.

Notes:

#137: When is a Good Time to Buy Stocks

Investors have a bad habit of overpaying for optimism. They run in and overpay because the "investor herd" is buying. Following the herd will not reap positive investment returns. It is a sucker bet. You will not get bargain prices on any investment without the presence of really bad news. Unfortunately, buying on bad news is psychologically a hard thing to do. But, whoever said investing was an easy game to play.

Notes:

#138: How Competent is the Federal Government

From Milton Friedman---"If you put the Federal Government in charge of the Sahara Desert, in five years there would be a shortage of sand." And you want the Federal Government to be in charge of your medical care? Are you nuts?

Notes:

#139: Is another Debt Jubilee Coming?

The ancient Babylonian kings would declare a debt jubilee when social unrest and conditions got dicey due to too much debt. This would wipe-out the debt of all borrowers and allow them to start off fresh. The economy could start over without the burden of debt depressing growth. Could we have a debt jubilee in the developed world to wipe-out the unsustainable levels of debt accumulated? The answer is yes, but it will come in a different shape and form. It will come in the form of the **Kondratiev Wave**. This is a 60 plus economic super cycle of credit expansion and destruction. The credit destruction phase (depression and hard times) lays the ground work for the next strong up phase carrying the economy to greater heights of technology and innovation. In other words, there must be credit liquidation before there can be another sustainable upswing.

Notes:

#140: TO BE BALANCED>>>NOT!

Everyone wants balance in their life. Yet balance, like security, does not exist in nature. To be in balanced is to be stagnant. **Stagnation over time produces nothing more than decline and decay.** Nature is always in movement and this movement is aggressive and chaotic. Your survival is dependent on understanding this simple truth.

Notes:

#141: HOW INFLATION WORKS

The guy who framed the first dollar he made 30 years ago in a 10 cent frame, now finds that today the frame is worth a dollar and the dollar is worth 10 cents.

Notes:

#142: LOVE AND MONEY

Money won't buy love but it will put a man in a good field position.

Notes:

#143: Mortals and the Path to Perfection

The only perfect thing about mortals is that they are perfectly imperfect. Perfection and mortals mix as well as water and oil. While mortals can be better, those who seek the path of perfection will have wasted their time on Earth. Accept your imperfections and rejoice in them. They are what make you unique. Everyone is different.

Notes:

#144: HOW POLITICIANS WILL ACT DURING MADDENING ECONOMIC TIMES

Harry Dent said it best::: *"In times of prolonged economic stress, politicians and central bankers won't bite the bullet. They won't accept short-term pain in return for long-term gains. Instead, they'll work to protect special interest groups and government budgets in the name of keeping people working and stopping any social unrest. Taxes will rise, not fall, and business regulations will increase, not drop"*.

Notes:

#145: MONEY=WEALTH (NOT)

MONEY is not wealth! It is simply a measure of wealth like a ruler measures length or a thermometer measures temperature. True economic wealth comes from giving individuals the tax incentives to work and invest for their futures.

Notes:

#146: THE NEW WELFARE DOLL

There is a now doll on the market called the "Welfare Doll". You wind it up and it doesn't work.

Notes:

#147: The Art of Planning by Mike Tyson

"Everybody has a plan until they get punched in the mouth"--Mike Tyson. We live in a business economy characterized by chaos & turbulence. It is not a question if something will go wrong but when. Have a backup plan and be liquid to take advantage of opportunities.

Notes:

#148: How Peace is Achieved?

Peace does not come from weakness….. but from strength and the willingness to project power. **The primary responsibility of the Federal Government is national defense and the security of the United States.**

Notes:

#149: BLINDNESS

Nothing is harder to see than the naked truth. **Big government is Not your friend; it is your competitor for Personal Power.**

Notes:

#150: HAS THE NAACP LOST ITS FOCUS?

The key for achieving success in life is obtaining a good education. Yet, why does the NAACP oppose the expansion of charter schools that the majority of minority parents desperately want. Charter schools have been one of the bright lights in raising educational standards for minority students. Minority parents, along with all parents, should be free from the clutches of failing union dominated public schools. The NAACP has lost its focus in not supporting an expansion of charter schools along with educational vouchers that will give minority parents choice of where to send their kids.

Notes:

#151: THE IMMORALITY OF NATIONS

Any country that does not give its citizens the incentives to save and invest for their futures has lost their moral compass. Without these incentives to save and invest for their better futures individuals will depend on the government for their wellbeing. They will become serfs of the state and will be under the yoke of government bondage. The **objective** of political policy should be to give individuals the incentives and opportunities to grow and prosper within the Rule of Law. Anything other than this will slowly eat away at the fabric of freedom and opportunity in American society.

Notes:

#152: How to end corporate cronyism

Do you seriously want to end corporate cronyism? I definitely do. Then, let's get rid of the corporate income tax. Corporations don't pay taxes---people do. The corporate income tax is passed on to a collective group of three. **The first** is higher prices to consumers for their goods and services. **The second** is reduced wages and benefits for their employees. **Lastly** is reduced dividends and capital appreciation for the stockholders. Let them keep the money and invest in new technologies and new businesses. Result>>new business formations=more high paying jobs and more tax revenue to government via the personal income tax.

Notes:

#153: HOW TO SEEK TRUE FREEDOM?

On a personal level there is no freedom unless you are financially free. Financially free means you are not heavily in debt and have enough savings to last you a year in an economic downturn. It would be smart not to depend on your employer for your only income, but have other "irons in the fire". No job is forever.

Notes:

#154: In the end how will governments deal with their massive debts?

Nothing goes on forever and that includes the rising mountain of government debt. Eventually a point is reach where the level of debt is unsustainable. Historically, how will governments deal with this glob of debt? Unable to service all this debt, governments will have no choice but to raise taxes, slash government benefits to the bone, crush pensions and confiscate portions of your wealth. Not a pretty picture, but there are no free lunches and all debt is repaid in some fashion.

Notes:

#155: How to Capitalize on Chaos

If you understand the Law of Entropy then all systems move from order to disorder or chaos. Not only am I talking about social economic systems, but also individual systems (namely you). Out of chaos comes opportunity. How do you capitalize on it? Simple, be liquid and have money in the bank. If you are heavily in debt and illiquid, financial opportunities will pass you by. Remember this concise statement>>> **"Liquidity is King—Not Elvis"**.

Notes:

#156: WHY A GOLD BASED DOLLAR?

There is a reason why gold has been the backing of currencies for 5,000 years. It puts leg irons on the whims of politicians to spend their countries into bankruptcy by issuing massive amount of debt. Eventually, the debt load becomes such a budgetary burden the country defaults and the debt bubble bursts and drags the economy down. A gold back dollar forces politicians to prioritize their spending. In the U.S., **the #1 priority of the Federal government is national defense and the security of the country.** Everything else follows that.

Notes:

#157: BAD POLICY=BAD POLICY

Bad economic policy, even for the best of reasons, is still bad policy.

Notes:

#158: Jobs! Jobs! & Jobs! Where do they come from?

Who creates the most jobs? More than 80% of new jobs created every year are created by companies less than five years old. To put it in another way, the genesis of job creation is the entrepreneurs.

Notes:

Lastly:

#159: WHEREIN LIES THE PROMISED LAND?

The Promised Land is that great land that lies between two mighty oceans (the Atlantic and Pacific). It is the land of opportunity—for growth and prosperity. It is for those individuals that want to be the helmsman of their own ship and not be under the yoke of government bondage. **It is the land of Freedom and Liberty.**

Notes:

Concluding Remarks

As I mentioned in the dedication, this book is devoted to free and independent thinkers everywhere. Never allow yourself to be controlled by any institution (secular or religious) that tells you how to live, think and act. You are the pilot of your own ship. You chart the course and must take the responsibility for your own actions.

May I suggest a symbol that will reinforce this uncomplicated philosophy. Wear a small sailboat on a necklace. This will be a reminder that you are the helmsman of your own ship. May you always be sailing into sunny horizons.

Sanford Kahn

www.ingramcontent.com/pod-product-compliance
Lightning Source LLC
Chambersburg PA
CBHW031050180526
45163CB00002BA/776